A FIRE AROSE FROM MY SOUL

MEMOIR OF FAITH

ANDREA WARDSWORTH BEASLEY

WestBow Press books may be ordered through booksellers or by contacting:

WestBow Press
A Division of Thomas Nelson & Zondervan
1663 Liberty Drive
Bloomington, IN 47403
www.westbowpress.com
844-714-3454

Because of the dynamic nature of the Internet, any web addresses or links contained in this book may have changed since publication and may no longer be valid. The views expressed in this work are solely those of the author and do not necessarily reflect the views of the publisher, and the publisher hereby disclaims any responsibility for them.

Any people depicted in stock imagery provided by Getty Images are models, and such images are being used for illustrative purposes only. Certain stock imagery © Getty Images.

Scripture quotations are taken from the Holy Bible, NEW INTERNATIONAL VERSION®, NIV® Copyright © 1973, 1978, 1984, 2011 by Biblica, Inc.® Used by permission. All rights reserved worldwide.

ISBN: 979-8-3850-1725-6 (sc)
ISBN: 979-8-3850-3183-2 (hc)
ISBN: 979-8-3850-1726-3 (e)

Library of Congress Control Number: 2024901902

Print information available on the last page.

WestBow Press rev. date: 08/13/2024

WESTBOW
PRESS®
A DIVISION OF THOMAS NELSON
& ZONDERVAN

Table of Contents

Preface

A FIRE AROSE FROM MY SOUL serves as a message of "FAITH" and "HOPE", as we find ourselves in life's challenges and the danger every day of our lives! It also serves as a **"Community *Call to Action Plan"*** and ***Personal Guide*** resulting from an epitomic **Family's flight before, during, and after a historical destroyer of all---*"A Fire*!"** Many people carry scars that others do not understand because they cannot visibly see them. This Book allows you to open wounds, communicate about knowledge, and provide wisdom needed to offer support prior to, or after any disaster that you can see, hear about, and feel led to do so. It is written from a *"Heart of Love"* offering a new hope to help you, and anyone who lives to witness a **Fire Disaster arise more spiritually, emotionally, and financially to rebuild and help others!**

After the **Biography about the Author**, there are some awesome **Collections of Poetic Interpretations offered by the Family**, which express their original first hand **"Up-close"** encounter of feelings that were seen, felt, smelt, and heard once the **"Hot Mess" Flames** ignited to turn into ***A Fire***! ***This Fire***, engulfed their entire lifestyle and personal belongings! The Poems expressed within this Book also disclose the sadness, hatred, disaster, love, and the responsibility shared by their Family, other individuals, and the nearby community. There are times in life when we may feel like our lives are reduced to *"Ashes"*. You will discover that Andrea makes references to the "HOT MESS" Flames that destroyed not only their belongings, but her life as she knew it before the House Fire. Remember, your needs may be great at that time, but **"Your troubles are TEMPORARY!" God loves you! Rise from your Fire! We Arose!**

Another purpose of this Book is to assist with a **mindset to build continued relationships** in order to make a better foundation to help other lives. We must MAKE THE TIME to learn how to communicate with one another, and effectively help other Families through the chaos, then offer supports to achieve more success after a Fire, or any other catastrophes. Disasters do warrant a time to draw nearer to others. The **dynamics** of *A Fire* Disaster are very, very challenging in all aspects. The Reflections in this text will help inform others about the **family challenges before, during, and after *A Fire***. Knowing of God's truth and character does help you overcome more obstacles and limitations. The described ***soul searching experiences of the Author's Family*** may clearly emphasize a direct and indirect process for the rebirth of a life and a family, as they...

"Arose like a Phoenix!"

This Book shares that it is important for all of us to be prepared and equipped for the work, social, and life skills to help oneself, one's family, and others. One must hold on to your faith and beliefs in God. The burnt and damaged pieces of your life are repairable, as we build more conversations to work together. Support your own and other families in need for a common good. Communities, Churches, and any Individual should come together during these times. It would be beneficial having a designed strategy within an organizational structure already in place to suggest what the next steps are after a disaster; to bring needy families into a better future. A pledge to educate and offer support will help ALL families *"Roll with the Punches of LIFE!" Prepare for your "Unexpected!"*

About the Author

Living Life Before the Fire

Living Life Before the Fire examines the LIFE of a single divorced Mom from Pineville, Louisiana born on December 12th one cold late Saturday evening around 11:57 PM. This nearly eight-pound baby girl, Andrea Marie Wardsworth was born to Anderson Wardsworth, Jr. from Natchitoches, LA and Mary Louise James Wardsworth from Pineville, LA. Her parents had two children, Andrea and a younger sister, Anna Gail. In the past, most babies were born in what was known then, as the *"Charity Hospital"* currently renamed the Huey P. Long Hospital. After Andrea's birth, her mother Mary grew very sick. Her mom readmitted herself to the hospital on a Sunday because the afterbirth from Andrea's birth remained in her Mother's womb, which could have easily caused an expediently quick death for her Mom. Both her parents were still in college at this time. Her Dad attended three years of college for the School of Art in Hawkins, Texas at Jarvis Christian College then later worked as an Offshore Cook, and had other jobs and businesses. He was an "Entrepreneur at Heart" owning a record shop, and a small fast food business off Lee Street called **Wings and Things.** *His food business featured a Fried Chicken Batter that her Dad created for his brother-friend, Julius W. Blazer, Jr. who owned a restaurant in Buffalo, New York.* Her Dad went to live with his friend for over a year to help him get his restaurant going. Anderson also made a specialty Pecan candy, as he loved to cook and draw! Her mother attended two Historical Black colleges in Louisiana; namely **Grambling State and Southern University and A&M College to obtain her Master's Degree**. Mary soon became a very valuable, loved, talented Chemistry Teacher, Community Leader, and Political Activist, as she loved helping many others achieve their personal and political goals throughout the Community.

Andrea's **Choctaw mixed Indian grandmother, Arizona "Zona" Davis James**, raised Andrea. Arizona was originally from *Tyrilley*, **Louisiana** (near the Colfax-Jena Area). The late Pastor Cousin Wardell Williams informed Andrea that this town was locked and gated, but does not exist anymore. The whereabouts of that key is still unknown. Arizona became the second wife to her **Avoyel Indian grandfather, Freeman. His birth name is Jean Pierre James** and Andrea's grandfather was later renamed Joseph "Freeman" James by his Momma, Cecile Solei or (Solie) when he arrived to Alexandria, Louisiana fleeing Mansura, Louisiana due to the death of his Dad, Levi James.

Barbara Jean Fisher; is Andrea's first Godmother and her mother's only sister as well. Barbara helped to raise Andrea and Anna alongside her currently living children, Val and Kevin. Barbara's baby girl, Montrena was not born during that time. They all lived together in their grandmother, Arizona "Zona's" white house on *"Kinfolk's Hill"* in Pineville, Louisiana, which still stands at 720 Sycamore Street currently in dire need of restoration now waiting to be remodeled. Arizona's two Uncles, Lee and Robert Torry built her Grandma's white wood framed house for **five hundred dollars!** Her grandmother had saved those five hundred dollars of her earnings by working as the House Maid, and as an adopted family member of a few "well-to-do" white families. The last favored family Zona worked for was the Leatherman Family in Pineville, Louisiana as she ironed, cooked, cleaned, raised, and fed their children. **During that time of the Century, a woman could not buy her own house, even though the house was constructed and paid for with her own hard-earned money**. Andrea was astonished to learn that a **"woman of color"** could not get a loan in her name on her own back then at any bank. Therefore, the house, which Arizona had built and paid cash for with her own wages, had to be purchased in her husband's name because that was the law of the land during that period. We were all one big happy family in that white house on the Kinfolk's Hill, as everyone lived with her Grandma Zona for a long while; at least six years after Andrea's birth. Aunt Barbara later remarried Uncle Ray Fisher who was in the military and moved away to Germany with her new husband adding the adorable new baby girl, Montrena to our close-knit family.

Andrea's memory recalls not liking her very early school years that much, as she did not want to separate from her Grandma Arizona's side at all! Little did she know at that time that the love for Education was ingrained in her makeup, due to the family of teachers who played very important roles in her early life. She attended a different elementary school every year during the late sixties until High School. She enjoyed those school experiences in the late seventies. Andrea was a cheerleader, on the Dance Line, on the Homecoming Court, an Honor Roll student, and amongst the Top Ten of the "Who's Who Amongst High School Students". Modeling fashions for The Hanger Department Store in the Alexandria Mall, and being a beauty pageant participant was also Andrea's hobby.

During this time, no one ever asked Andrea what she wanted to be. She never knew or discussed any occupational fields for a possible job after High School. High School was simply a trial and error hit, or miss series of events. Completing her education was a successful stream of events. Andrea attended Louisiana State University in Alexandria (LSUA). She boldly joined the Army Reserves the first summer of her college enrollment, after discussing it with her Recruiter; Uncle Ray Fisher. Then, she headed off to Fort McClellan, Alabama for Basic Training. When Andrea returned from the Army's Basic Training program, she enrolled at the University of Louisiana (ULL), then called (USL) in Lafayette, Louisiana. She completed her Bachelor of Science degree in Business Administration at midterm and worked as a Department Manager Trainee at J. C. Penney's Department Store. Andrea Marie Wardsworth first married at the age of 29, and had her first child at 30. Her last of the five children was born at the age of 40; *a ten-year span in this order; Alex, Austen, Asa, Ayanna, and Abram.* Although Andrea had some good memories raising her children during her first marriage, she went through a very difficult and much harder time trying to make ends meet on her own while married with five children. She divorced and was single mom when the oldest child turned thirteen years of age. It was during this first marriage that she found Jesus for herself---not by accident, but out of a real yearning necessity, as she searched for something bigger and better in life than a constant struggle and unhappy marriage. Years later, she and her children awoke to the much bigger battle...***A House Fire***!

Living Life During A Fire

***Living Life During A Fire* was HARD!** The Fire destroyed the little that Andrea had left---*things that she had worked so hard to gain, after her divorce from her children's father seemed unimaginably **as hard as the Hell** mentioned in the Bible!* However, Andrea comes from a long lineage of *strong willed women*! She literally toted her four-year old son, Abram in her arms, as she and her other four kids walked down the street of a **dusk to dawn despair to find a safe shelter**. The family car was in the driveway parked and the car keys were in Andrea's purse still inside the burning house. In a panic, Andrea asked her oldest son, Alex to run back inside the house to get her purse in the kitchen. Thank God, he was able to get in and out in time from that smoke! The *Fire* trucks had arrived excessively **late** though! **All was lost by smoke and smell!** The "Hot Mess" Flames from the house had damaged the car engine also. It did not start! The house burned from the inside out leaving only the outside brick shell! Andrea remembered crying to God for help the very night **before the Fire**! Yes, the night **before the Fire** she began bearing her soul in desperation, as she squatted on the bathroom floor of the small three-bedroom one bath house she rented **the night before retiring for bed, then awakening to *the Fire early that morning*! Her second son, Austen woke them up just in time to flee their burning beds**! So she and the kids moved in with her parents immediately afterwards. The Fire Marshal stated that he would send someone else over within a couple of days to seek evidence for the cause of **the Fire.** It was determined that the cause was an electrical fire after the questioning process began in search of more clues behind how the Fire started. Before the other Fire Inspector could come out to reexamine the situation, the Owner of the property had already sent his own workers over to the house. They completely "gutted" the property! **Why was that?** Thankful for being alive, Andrea and her children walked away from *"A Fire that Arose from Her Soul Cry to God!"* Andrea later asked. **"What's next Lord! What is next?"...Life is so full of surprises!**

Living Life Because of the Fire

Living Life Because of the Fire was a Miracle of Happenings! Andrea received a call from an Alexandria Town Talk Newspaper Reporter who reported the news about their House Fire Disaster in the local Daily Town Talk after the Fire. The Reporter telephoned Andrea stating that their Manager was contacted by a television show that broadcasted in New York, and that Show was trying to get in touch with Andrea and her family. ***"BUT Why?"*** she asked. She discovered that they wanted to see if they could schedule an appearance for Andrea to come on their TV Show. Actually, two TV Shows initially contacted Andrea to request her personal appearance,

The Montel Williams Show and The Life and Styles Show. Neither of these two shows are broadcasted on TV anymore. Andrea responded to the Reporter, ***"What did you say?"*** She could not believe it! No one in the Family could believe it --- **A full Four-Day All Expense Paid Trip to New York on the Life and Styles TV Show**. Andrea chose this Show because they offered to give her a "Makeover" that she desperately felt she needed then at that time**. She wanted to feel better about her life and herself!** *She wanted to feel more beautiful from her state of depression and stress.* **This was a total miracle from God in Andrea's mind. She hung up the phone and still could not believe the conversation that had just taken place until the evidence of the actual tickets to fly to New York City arrived by certified mail!** Out of all the millions, and billions, and trillions of News Stories, "Lexus Nexus" selected her Family's News Story to report! It was unimaginable that Chronicles of Andrea and her children's story and journey through the scorching "HOT MESS FLAMES" was a story worthy to tell! Andrea wanted both of her two older sons to go with her, but she had to choose only one, as she could not afford to pay for and extra airplane ticket. She and her oldest son, Alex got on the airplane once they received the tickets. They flew off to New York leaving Austen, Asa, Ayanna, and Abram home with her parents. She did not know what to expect. She did not know how to act. The plane had landed. It was dark when they arrived at the airport. They found and claimed their baggage, then stepped off the escalator to see a man holding a sign high above his head, which read, **"THE LIFE AND STYLES TV SHOW".** They followed him towards the white limousine and received the instructions to check into the hotel, put away their bags, eat, and get ready to leave again, so that she could try on clothes for a dress rehearsal that same night after the flight..."WOW!" It all was happening so fast! It all sounded so exciting, and they were still riding in a white limousine! Arriving at their next destination, a young woman greeted them. Her job was to assist Andrea to find a nice wardrobe for the live TV Show Production the next day. This activity took a while and was a lot of work. The woman kept pulling out dressy business clothes, and kept trying to find Andrea some dress heels to wear on the TV Show for the next day. Everything happened so quickly. Andrea stepped out of the classy white limousine to the hotel and arrived in New York City wearing a gray pair of used sweat pants, gray jacket and black boots. She really really felt like she looked a **"HOT MESS!" You will be able to view some of the "Hot Mess Photos" of images inside their burnt rental home towards the end of this Book**. Tomorrow, she would have a better outfit to wear! Her son, Alex was there waiting patiently until the "finding a nice outfit" task was completed.

Andrea ending up agreeing to wear an outfit, which included a tea-length, flared teal green full skirt, black open toe three-inch heels with a matching short sleeve teal green blouse and a long ruffled teal green scarf. Andrea also noticed that this young woman was stapling the receipts of the clothing she chose to wear on the paper on her clipboard. This was a ***"so real" business moment***. Andrea made many mental notes in her mind about how ***this moment seemed like a real job*** she was not at all familiar with, and it also seemed fun to see how they operated since fashion merchandising was her first love and an occupational dream job; to be a Buyer. After that almost two-hour evening ordeal, she was so tired and ready to go back to the hotel to sleep. They were also hungry again after the driver dropped them back off to the hotel, so they walked down that same street to a sandwich shop, since the driver had also provided them with some money to spend for their food. This was really a first class operation! Andrea was so glad that she had her older son with her, but she wished that she could have afforded to take Austen, her second son as well. Alex seemed very confident of himself on the trip, and she was very proud of how he was handling himself in the unfamiliar territory of New York City at sixteen years of age. The next day they had to get up early again to film *The TV Show*. They arrived at the Studio and the scene that they saw with the *LIVE* audience clapping was a "Wowing Experience!" This was such a ***"For REAL"*** experience! A person standing in the audience held up a sign cueing the audience what to do, and when. She saw another young man interviewing **Kimora Lee Simmons, a fashion model, writer, and affiliate of Baby Phat.** Yes, Kimora Lee who stood about 5'10" without heels walked right past the 5'6 and a half inch "Self" of Andrea Marie Wardsworth Baker at that time from Alexandria, Louisiana in her high heels. Her son, Alex was standing "front and center" enjoying every view of every person involved and the exhilarating very fast paced atmosphere!

Andrea later learned that the young man interviewed by **Kimora Lee was Farrah Gray, a young Millionaire**! He was telling his story of how he started, as a young Entrepreneur by making his Grandma's syrup. The Story was interesting and caught Andrea's attention because she had already started using and making her own grandmother Zona's Pear Preserve Recipe at home with her own twist to the Recipe to make for others to give away as gifts! She began to feel like God's Plan for her life was being revealed more and more quickly each day now, so Andrea began to pay more attention to the many personal details of his Interview briefly prior to her own name being called to enter the Stage for her own personal Interview, then to later be whisked away, and quizzed about her own personal hair and makeup needs.

Just as they scooted Andrea into the high-backed chair for make-up, in walks **Mikki Taylor, the Essence Magazine Editor, and Beauty Advisor**! Andrea discovered that Mikki had been with Essence Magazine for many years and she gave Andrea her personal business card for future reference, which Andrea lost during her travel back home to Alexandria, Louisiana. Andrea suddenly felt as though she was of instant "Celebrity" status! She felt like she was a "***Person of Interest to the* WORLD**!" They shared a great conversation, as Mikki wanted to know more about Andrea and her five children. Andrea appeared to be so at ease with the TV Production that even Mikki was engrossed in the personal conversation with Andrea. **Mikki even mentioned that it seemed like the personal encounter they were having right then at that exact time and place seemed like a true *"Divine Connection"* meant to be**! Anyway, Mikki asked Andrea how she wanted her hair to look. All Andrea could reply in that moment was that she **"*wanted pretty brown hair.*"** There was no time to give Andrea the longer hair extensions that she really wanted, so the beautician had to make do with her own natural hair for the Show. The Beautician was able to add some highlighted shorter extensions to her natural dark brown hair for the new makeover look. Andrea quickly received a script of what the Directors wanted her to say only moments before it was time for her to walk out on the platform in front of the TV camera for their *LIVE* production. Andrea responded that the task would be very simple for her to do, as it seemed so natural for her to be there. The time had finally arrived for the lights, the camera, and the ***ACTION!*** Andrea walked out on the stage, modeled, smiled, and made eye contact by looking from side to side at the audience, as she glided across that platform stage with ease like a professional model! ***She received an outstanding applause, which she will NEVER forget!*** Everything seemed so very familiar with appearing before an audience because she had modeled before during High School. Andrea surprisingly was in her element for a moment! Anyway, Mikki again asked Andrea how she wanted her hair to look. All Andrea could reply again was that she *"wanted pretty brown hair!"* Then, the questions came forth from the Host of the TV Show. Andrea realized again that she really did feel so at ease. The story and the new *dramatization of her Family's plight from the House **Fire** was still surreal. Her act (as they* knew it there during the Interview) was *NOT* an act. She had actually lived through it and could retell her Family Story. This Story of the single mother of five who survived a total ***Fire***

Disaster was to be aired on a National television syndication between commercial breaks with the "Before and After" camera shots about a month later. Astoundingly, in that instance, the TV Host renamed Andrea from being a single Mom with five children who was very devastated by **the *Fire*** to being ***"A Rising Phoenix Who Arose from the Ashes, and Lived through the Fire!"*** *Andrea replayed that title again in her mind... A Phoenix who AROSE from the ashes, and LIVED through the Fire!*

Andrea and her children did eventually **"Arise from Ashes and Lived through the *Fire*"** however; she still did not feel good at all about her present situation. She did not have her own house for her kids or herself to live in! ***In fact, it took years to RECOVER!*** Many of those feelings of a lack of security came back periodically year after year after year! Andrea was very surprised to receive a gift certificate to the Nest Spa for herself in Alexandria, Louisiana, and a two thousand dollar gift certificate to The Alexandria Mall, so that she could take her children shopping when she and Alex returned home to Alexandria, Louisiana by the Life & Styles TV Show. She was shocked and *so grateful* because they were still *so very* needy. ***Andrea graciously received and accepted the two thousand dollars, but the gift actually felt like one drop of water in an empty gallon bucket! They were "drowning!"*** People just do not realize how much it costs to take care of, and support a family of five children, especially as a single divorced female parent. One job was ***NEVER*** enough! Yet, Andrea still had always considered herself *so blessed* to have her *quiver* full with her five children and their future worth of children according to God's written WORD would be immeasurable ***eventually***!

Here are some astounding facts. The food costs for low to middle-income families represents the second largest expenditure. Families in the North spend the most on child-related expenditures while those in Rural and Southern areas spend the least. Finally, just to give you an idea, when Andrea started writing this Story, she read that single parents spend approximately seven percent (7%) less on their children than husband-wife pairs, although this represents a larger share of their total income. So what does it cost to raise a child from birth to age 17? Well, when Andrea actually started writing this book in July 2011, the average cost was about $12,941.18 per year based on a $220,000 cost for raising a child for seventeen years. Families in the low-income group could anticipate spending $205,960 to raise a child; the middle-income group will spend approximately $286,050 to accomplish this task, and the high-income group will spend about $475,680 on a child until he or she reaches 17. These figures are astounding when you see them on paper! *It is so much MORE NOW*! (Andrea's Family Plight is another "real life example" that God surely provides!) *Andrea sought this information in the US Department of Agriculture Calculator when she first started writing this Book!* Again, *these costs ARE higher now*! Andrea and her family had lost over twenty thousand dollars of goods and wares in that **House Fire**! She attempted to replace some of the clothes and material things for her children as much as possible, and soon discovered that this was an endless task! She could not physically complete this parental function making thirty-four thousand a year on a teacher's salary! She was only one parent supporting her children who needed medical, dental, and health services as well. On top of that, the bills were coming in for items that they no longer owned; *a result of the Fire*, and she needed to repurchase those same items. It was absurd trying to repair her credit! There was **NO** money to save! There were **NO** summer trips taken, **NO** movies, and **NO** dating for Mamma...**NO NO** nothing for years! Yes, "years of celibacy and tears", but who knew....**she was just trying to make her ends meet by a *"huff and a puff, and a prayer!"*** Talk about a living nightmare! ***Andrea truly felt like she was locked away in a dungeon with no key!*** No one knows what a person goes through, even though there is a smile on his or her face unless you have had the same experience for yourself. She was literary **STUCK** in her Parent's Home! ***This is one story of survival she needed to report to raise more awareness* and *help someone else up out of the Fire to arise as a Phoenix because this was the "REAL DEAL" Honest to God Truth of a Living Witness to a Survival!***

After the taping of The TV Show, Andrea returned to the hotel, looked out the window of that hotel room, and noticed a dance studio. She and her son, Alex realized then, at that moment that they were really truly in ***New York, New YORK***! They desired to have a great time their last night in New York City, so they left the hotel and started walking down the streets of New York in January. It was a very, very cold night, but they did not care. They wanted to walk down Times Square, see the bright lights that they saw on TV, and they were getting hungry. She and Alex caught the subway train to get where they needed to go. They had no clue about how to enter the subway but they knew that they had to get a token to enter and ride the train. There was a police officer on the streets who offered them more directions. That police officer rather laughed at Andrea for not knowing how to enter the subway gate to get on the train. Alex kind of stepped up and took over to lead his Mom on their night tour of New York City after they got off the train.

Andrea noticed a woman walking her baby in a stroller covered in a clear heavy plastic wrap. The light brownish snow appeared to drag on the streets, as cars pushed the dirty snow to the side of the street curbs. She noticed there were some vehicles along the streets, which had not moved or been driven in a long while. It seemed like everyone was walking at a very fast pace down the streets of New York. There were shops everywhere on every corner. Andrea concluded in that instant that she wanted the rest of her children to have a trip together one day to New York. ***"The Big* Apple"** calls their names for at least for one more visit in her lifetime, as a Family. **New York was a very busy city that you do not want to be lost in, but still you would want to see all the many things that it has to offer during the springtime, once all the snow melts.** Andrea said that *one day* in the future she would want to experience a Broadway play, look at the waterfront, shop for clothing bargains, and visit the Morning Star for breakfast and Hell's Kitchen at night. They finally reached their destination. The first shop they came to was a sports shop---***well, they were window-shopping!*** As they moved further down the street and stood in Times Squares, **Andrea twirled full circle in the middle of the street; arms outstretched and looked chin-up to the sky to look at all the brightly lit huge billboard signs and sky like a child! It was a very magical moment for her!** She was in New York, New York and wanted to come back to visit there one more time to see more things! Eventually, they strolled upon a Red Lobster Restaurant; a place that they were familiar with. They ordered, ate, and starting noticing the people of New York. ***The people looked just like them; very regular and ordinary!*** The food was good and they ate it **ALL** then, Andrea started to feel nauseated and ran to the bathroom to throw it all up! Maybe, Andrea ate too fast! Her stomach could not take the rich lobster and shrimp in that butter sauce. Her life was still so stressful! It could have been all the excitement as well. She was not use to eating a full stomach of much food since ***the Fire*** happened, as her body had not fully recovered from the stress of it all yet, and would not recover for many months later. Well, so much for her Tour of the *"City That Never Sleeps"!* They found the subway train again and made it back safely to the hotel dead tired, and ready to sleep. When they awoke the next morning, they did not have the limousine on the return trip home, but the ride was still comfortable. The fairy tale trip had ended, and the venture was officially over. WOW! The trip was actually more work that Andrea had ever expected. It was a bittersweet experience for her once they were back on the airplane heading back home to Alexandria, Louisiana. She had much appreciation for the temporary Stardom.

Andrea also realized that being a Star takes a lot of work to maintain the image, lifestyle, and busy schedule all the time!

After some time elapsed, Andrea also helped to provide direct care to her grandmother at night, because one day her Grandma Arizona had attempted to throw a heavy homemade quilt from her bed to the nearby chair in her bedroom, causing her to fall. Her Grandmother "Zona" lived alone at that time, and was doing very well living in her own house by herself until her grandmother had that fall causing her to fracture a small bone in her neck. Andrea again found herself again saying, *"What next Lord? What is next?"* This incident of the fall caused Andrea's Grandmother's health to decline quicker. *Grandmother Arizona eventually caught pneumonia and died fifteen days shy of being one hundred years old. She was the first-born and last to die of her fourteen siblings to her parents; Benjamin "Ben" Davis and Alice Briggs.*

Andrea had not prepared herself for her grandma's death at all! After her grandmother's death, Andrea began to search her own self and soul again. She sought more answers about her own inheritance through God. She knew she was not a quitter. She had to support herself and her children financially more now than ever before, as her mental health support person and guide; her beloved grandmother Zona was gone! Andrea made a choice right then to live alone and not remarry until her children were *almost grown and gone*, as she had heard unfavorable stories about the **"extra stresses"** of dating, mixing, and blending of families from her Grandma and other close friends. It was reported that it was not an easy task to be a Stepparent because we are all raised differently when young. Surroundings are different. Only the strong survive, so be up for the task. Andrea was not at that point in her life. Has anyone heard that? Has anyone else heard that? At that time, Andrea realized she was just not cut out for any extra stresses or emotional work! She just wanted to focus on what she was already comfortable with---**her own children and earning a good living!** She had heard and learned **that it is still written in the Word of God that an inheritance is left for the children's children, as Proverbs 13:22 reads "that a good man leaves an inheritance for his children's children, and a sinner's wealth is stored up for the righteous."** Andrea also began to wonder about the images and teachings that had already been imprinted, and established in her through her grandmother's teachings. She started thinking about the favorite things and lessons she remembered about being around her grandmother, so she began making her grandmother's specialty cake and preserving pears from her memories of seeing her grandmother Arizona in the kitchen. She even planted two pear trees to have a crop of her own organic pears on her own property, so she could stop looking for other people who had a pear tree in their yard! Andrea started sharing the homemade desserts; cake and banana pudding with others and family members; and came up with the name **ZONA'S PLACE!** She designed a monthly Calendar in her Grandmother's honor featuring art of pears, as well! The pear is a favored fruit symbol Andrea uses in the Calendar in honor of her Grandma Arizona homemade pear preserves!

Living Life After the Fire

***Living life after the Fire* had certainly been another Desperate Challenge!** The Thanksgivings and Christmases thereafter without her Grandmother Arizona seemed to have lost much of their very charming family entertainment appeals. Still unsatisfied with her financially bleak picture, Andrea decided to continue her pursuit of education by obtaining a Master's Degree, which only bumped her Teacher salary up by **about $40.00 a month!** *(This should say a lot about the present shameful Teacher salaries in Louisiana and poverty levels!)* However, Andrea graduated on December 12, 2009, on her Fiftieth Birthday, with a Master's Degree in the Arts of Teaching from Louisiana Christian University in Pineville, Louisiana! Without unwavering courage, Andrea continued to move forward. She still had a great courage and strength about her. Some talk about their destiny and life paths; Andrea definitely knew she was on an important part of her divine path when her graduation day was actually on her birthday! Some things are just not by chance. It is destiny!

Andrea's ideas began to FLOW! She later also piloted and produced a Testimonial Talk Show in April of 2010 calling it ***"THE AROSE TV SHOW"* (AROSE is the acronym for "A Reproduction of Saintly Experiences.")** Others may still view the beginning short clips of THE AROSE TV SHOW on the YouTube site on the Internet. Her TV Show shared local testimonies about the lives of ordinary people in the community and businesses to promote a public good will. She also originally designed and idea and started **"ZONA'S PLACE.** *It was a* means to offer the education of the art and ole time craft of preserving fruit, provide tips about the benefits of having your own garden in a rural community, and provide information about the food necessary to keep desired animals in their natural habitats around your area and back yard, but not the snakes. Andrea remembers going to the Petrus Feed Store to get the ingredients to make her own batch of Snake-Away product! As stated previously, she designed a self-published ***ZONA'S PLACE Calendar*** for close family and friends highlighting her Grandmother Arizona, as the "***Mother of Many***"! The starter businesses Andrea did start were short-lived because she did not have the time nor finances to continue to fund them by herself and raise her children. Maybe one day she will start reprinting the ***ZONA'S Place Calendar***! She would bake for her Family mostly, but did have some special Holiday requests for her delicious Pineapple Butter four layer cake topped with a pecan cross and Banana Pudding! Andrea mentioned that her daughter, Ayanna is doing such a great job baking for the Family now during the Holidays! Although Andrea remained very involved with her own children all the time by offering them much love, support, and encouragement, she also worked as a part-time Counselor to help other at-risk youth for five years with a Counseling Agency. She also studied to become a REALTOR in the State of Louisiana. Today, Andrea lives happily remarried since July 24 of 2021; now known as Mrs. Andrea Wardsworth Beasley seventeen years after the **Fire**! She stated that marriage is a divine daily work of **"Love in Progress!"** Unlike driving a car, close your eyes and allow God to be the **"Driver"** in your marriage even when things appear to break down that you do not understand. The Marriage Road may appear curvy at times, but you stay straight and only listen for **God's Instructions** on when to stop or move forward about what to do, even though you may seek advice from a certain family or a close friend. Then, stay true and happy for yourself! **Keep God first!** Her vivid **Fire** memories, which caused hurt, stress and depression does tend to linger at times, yet she feels so blessed to be able to live and tell her own story TODAY! Andrea remarried at the age of 61.

Andrea maintains her current membership of **www.realtor.com,** and **www.zillow.com.** Andrea actually had a ***dream*** about being a Real Estate Agent also ***after the Fire***, which prompted her to seek the requirements to become a licensed real estate agent. **The next day after her Dream to be a REALTOR to help many others achieve their own dream goals of homeownership she achieved her GOAL!** Now, you can truly "***ASK FOR ANDREA!***" **She passed the National and State of Louisiana Realtor Exam to help you with your Louisiana Real Estate needs!** ***The Fire pushed her through with strength to work three jobs until her own Dream of Homeownership prevailed to become her own REALITY for over twenty years!*** She always loved to write books and poetry in her spare time. Andrea was truly led, and inspired to tell her story by releasing her story ideas through the "Art of Writing"! Andrea smiled when her new husband Charles mentioned that it seems that her ***"Brain is on Fire at times!" Andrea has ideas that really come to life and happen! She still rises early most days to write and make her checklists for the day. Where does the energy come from? ...The Holy Spirit!***

Other Books

In summary, ***Andrea states that she speaks them into existence! She believes the Word of God and has Faith!*** **She prays that this Inspirational Book inspire YOU as WELL! ...*A FIRE AROSE FROM MY SOUL MEMOIR OF FAITH* is a** TRUE TESTIMONY of her Family's Flight from a Fire. Andrea prides herself as being a Christian Author and has other Books as well to offer you in her Collection along with **A FIRE AROSE FROM MY SOUL MEMOIR OF FAITH.**

Other Book Titles influenced by Christian principals and offered by Andrea Wardsworth Beasley wrote for publishing are as follows:

- *A HANDFUL OF LIFE*; **a Book of Inspirational Poems about the different stages, phases, and encounters of Life that are a Masterpiece of original principles, thoughts and feelings through Living Poetry!**

- *MY MAMMA GOT FREAKY HAIR*; **a delightful Children's book about a young girl named Johanna and the screaming love relationship with her Mom who is dying of Cancer, as she expresses what she sees and feels by looking at her Mom's uniquely wild hair. She sings and prays to God.**

- **Three beautifully colored "THEMED" Tracing and Coloring Activity Books for All Children entitled, *TRACING UNDER THE SEA For All Kids, TRACING FROM EARTH TO SPACE For All Kids, and TRACING IN THE JUNGLE For All Kids.* Children must practice using and holding a pencil to develop proper skills for writing fundamentals using favored items and words of objects known about the Sea, Earth, Space and the Jungle that kids will LOVE!**

- *AYANNA LOVES LOVES DOMINO The Story;* A Children's Love Story about a young girl and her new adopted pet kitten named "Domino" brought to her home during COVID-19. Pet Therapy works for many people including depressed children and adults! Domino has a Superpower; THE CAT CAN FLY and Ayanna prayed for that Kitten!

- *The AYANNA LOVES LOVES DOMINO ACTIVITY BOOK;* The AYANNA LOVES LOVES DOMINO original Story with Activity Pages that include some primary math problems, writing exercises, and great Activities for Children.

- *HEALED - A Personal Food and Medical History Journal*; documents your own personal diary of daily food intake. It also highlights the *Foods of Slaves and Indians,* as well as the Author's account of prominent very common health issues such as Cholesterol, Gout, Gall Stones, and High Blood Pressure from her own personal journey and family health history with a Holistic approach. A Gumbo and Jambalaya Recipe are included in this Book.

- *CONNECTIONS Until We Part To Another Life;* A Trust, Will and Estate Planning Guide made simple for you to keep forever in your Family used to "Connect the pieces of your personal life" using charts and tables for you and your Family members to use and complete prior to death for your loved ones.

- *UPCLOSE BECAUSE OF YOU Journals;* beautiful Journals designed with you in mind with vivid colors for the Daughters, Sons, Moms, Dads and a Self-Journal for everyone with 180-215 pages! "These make great GIFTS!"

- *ANIMAL FRIENDS SEEN ON THE ROAD TO LOUISIANA;* A Children's Fiction "rhyming" story about a child's recollection of the events of the more popular Animals known to inhabit the State of Louisiana and seen during his ride down the Louisiana Road to get to New Orleans, Louisiana for the Mardi Gras with his Mom and family.

- *The ZONA'S PLACE Calendar;* a 12 Month Inspirational Calendar with filled with Art of Pears.

  ***Request this purchase through Website or Email.

  Website: www.aroseenterpriseenterperisesllc

  Email: AroseEnterprises1@gmail.com

- *The "BAM" Card;* a note card of information to display above your car visor to remind you of what to do in the event you are stopped by a Police Officer.

  ***Request this purchase through Website or Email.

  Website: www.aroseenterpriseenterperisesllc

  Email: AroseEnterprises1@gmail.com

Continue to Follow Andrea Wardsworth Beasley on her website for any updates and stay current with her latest books. Writing Poetry and Children's Books are her favorites. Enjoy the captivating spirited journey rebuilt and rediscovered through Andrea's Books today!

Andrea wants you to remember to *"Fight the Good Fight of Faith" to win this Race of LIFE.* Reach out to feel love and compassion when necessary. Help others survive a FIRE, or any other Disaster! Remember that sometimes we deliberately have to push away sorrow to "CHOOSE LIFE"! Please share her Testimony! Run and Tell it! Cry when you need to! Get back up, and then roll with the punches! Your Life will not be reduced to "ASHES"!

"Choose LIFE!" Choose LIFE! Choose LIFE!"

Introduction

The Story

Austen (the second oldest son) runs into his mom's bedroom and says, "Mamma, the house is full of SMOKE!" His Mom (Andrea) responds, "Where is the Fire? ---- LOOK, it is right near your bed! ---The curtains are on FIRE!" Andrea stated, *"We were as Fireflies! We were dancing in distress as we arose from…the love-hate relationship encountered, as flight victims of our house because of the Fire.* I would say that the devil really attempted to take us out after my last son, Abram was born. That house *Fire* destroyed all that we had at 2:00 AM in the morning, during the end of October! Needless to say, **WE DID NOT** have a good Thanksgiving or Christmas! I also realized I sent my oldest son back into the burning house to see if he could find my car keys and purse! **(*Well, I had never been in that type of trauma ever before and did not realize what I was asking Alex, my oldest son to do. He is our very brave Hero also! I just knew that we needed a car and the things in my purse.*) My mind and stomach were in knots!** You never think anything will ever happen to you if you have been in a safe and sheltered environment most of your life, but prepare now! The night before the *Fire* after I bathed my two youngest children, Ayanna and Abram I sat on the floor of that small bathroom, and cried and yelled to God to help get us out of that rent house! It was too small. My kids needed more space. The youngest kids favorite playtime was in the bathtub, as we pretended they were in a ship full of toys. I wanted to live in the present with a great new start without living with anymore grief! I would have gladly left Louisiana if there was any new hope at all to go somewhere else! I was feeling so alone*! I felt that there was no one physically here in a body that could help us at all on this Earth to transport me to another Life quick!*

Anyway, luckily for us, my second son, Austen is another *HERO* to us! He woke us all up snug in our beds during that **Fire** because he was awakened by his Angel sent by God! *(Now, this is my own personal opinion that it was an Angel, but I bet Austen would say the same thing too!). An Angel in the Bible has many purposes. They were messengers, protectors, and agents of God's Will by carrying out tasks on God's behalf by sending messages and guidance. In other words, Angels are Facilitators of God's Plan to help HUMANS align themselves to God's Will!* God heard my prayer and knew our needs! My son, Alex was the last one awakened, as he lay dreaming about rescuing a running teen from the Devil's snatch with his hook. (He shared that with us later and I asked him to draw me a picture of his dream. He did, but I cannot find the drawing now). Remember, although evil forces attempt to break up families any kind of way that he can, we were **NOT** supposed to perish that morning! At this very moment, as I retell **the Fire** story, I reminded myself of the real human person *Thief* that had come into our home a year before the **Fire**! The robber was a young man riding a bicycle. He broke the back window of our house and entered through the kitchen while everyone was away at work and school. He stole many of our possessions. The police searched and looked for him. I prayed for our things to return to us, but all I really wanted back was the collection of the old big silver dollar coins my grandmother had saved for us over the years and given me, so I could pass them down to my children from her. I also wanted my favorite black hooded leather jacket back that I had bought from the Montgomery Wards, a favorite department store of mine at that time, which is no longer in operation in Alexandria, Louisiana. Some of you may remember that store. I just loved that jacket! It was so warm and at that time, I had not seen another real leather jacket like that before with a hood on it. **I had saved my nickels and dimes to buy the black leather hooded coat**! I was so excited to be able to make that purchase MINE! I just yearned for something nice for myself; a nice coat to wear that winter because I usually spent all I had on my children. A *Thief* took those things without permission. **The Thief** did end up being a young man who was riding through the neighborhood to visit his Aunt who lived in the house around on the other street of our residence on a bicycle. *(A police officer reported later that this young man would ride around on his bike, and then* *look to check out the houses and the residents in the area neighborhood.)* Everyone on my street worked. I am sure the *Thief* noticed when everyone would leave the home to develop his plan to rob us. He broke the kitchen window in the back, entered the kitchen, walked down the hall of our home, and **TOOK our possessions**; things that he could easily get money for. **Well, that Human *Thief* was caught!** We got our first dog after that; Rocky the Rottweiler! I compare that Human *Thief* to the **Fire** *now*, as I write because that **Fire** rummaged through all of our things, as well. The only difference between the two things was that ***the physical Fire took and destroyed ALL!*** Through it all, I still had to focus and I did refocus! I had to believe that GOD still had a great Plan for **OUR** lives although everything smelled burnt and looked burnt! Anything small that could be salvaged had the burnt smell on it, which we did not want to bring back into any house! Burnt items really stink badly!

I did not fully realize God's plan then. I do realize more of the plan now, even as I write this Story! I did not COLLAPSE! I still had a purpose! That is why after the *Fire* I felt I had to mentally learn to breathe in *FRESH* air again. I was even more determined to get back what we had lost! I wanted to know and learn what it was that GOD wanted us collectively to do, and *ME* alone to do. We ended up living with my parents because ***I had enough sense to know that if we did not have a penny extra before the Fire***, ***we definitely had less than a penny after the Fire***! We also needed to repurchase everything including underwear. I could not afford an apartment or another rent house. We did not even have clean underwear for the next day. I was so stressed and nervous, and ashamed that I could not even eat much for first three weeks or four weeks after the *Fire*. **There was stress coming from all angles!** My parents were stressed having all of us in their home. My sister was asking when I would get back in a house by myself. We did go live with my sister for a few months. Living with others **--- Well, *it was just NOT the same as having you own space. Seeing the house we use to live in was simply a skeletal shell reminder of the life we once knew, and more troubles to go through! All our cherished photos, and childhood toys were swallowed up by the merciless flames!*** I really did not want to apply for government housing and thank God there is a system to help those that need that assistance called, 'Welfare" or "Government Housing!" At that time, the Government houses were limited in good areas. I knew instinctively and intuitively that my children needed more structure since I was a single parent. I knew I did not want or need my children; especially the four boys in a setting where they were home alone when I was not there, so they would not get into trouble. Although our homeless situation was not my fault, I was very frustrated! I would cry and ask God daily what else I needed to do, and to help me help my kids understand that the money we really needed may never get to us fast enough to take care of our immediate needs the way we really needed it to with one job! Yet, we were so grateful for everything, and anything given us from anyone, and for my parents for allowing us to stay there. ***My physical body went into some kind of state that I had never ever felt before. Food had no taste in my mouth. I just did not want much food. I did not get much sleep either! It must have been my nerves. It was also stress! It was the mind working overtime with questions and the rehearsal of fears,*** as I was looking back at the past and the present year. I would stay up late at night and write things. I wanted to focus on forming my own business. It was an attack of evil bringing on a depression, but ***I never did let my children see me CRY, HOLLER, OR SCREAM the real way I felt on the inside! I WAS CRYING*** on the ***INSIDE MANY DAYS!*** They were too young to understand my feelings, or how I hurt being in a hopeless situation. I would lock myself in the bathroom. The bathroom is where I felt God's presence. **There was *NO NOISE THERE!* I could close my eyes behind a locked door for five to fifteen minutes and not be found in my own despair of silence! I would meet with GOD right there in the bathroom and *HE* would give me inspirational ideas!** Where in the world was the money going to come from for these ideas? I could not think of myself as "POOR ME." I had children that depended on ME! Well, the time must be right NOW! I did self-talk, "Do what you can a little at a time. Make one step forward at a time!" **I learned to pay attention to more details regarding e-v-e-r-y-thing when I felt spiritually connect to something! The enunciations of sounds to my ears from the words I heard became clearer as I drove down the street one day on Horseshoe Drive.** All I can say is that prayers do work! My head (chin up) began to ***lift upward towards the sky again a little bit more each day and get through the day!*** I made sure I brought my children to church and although we all were baptized before, we asked the Pastor to baptize us ***again*** at **The WORD Christian Center** on Lee Street in Alexandria, Louisiana. Our Pastors and the entire church congregation were there for us! The Community support we received was there also, as our televised Story aired on the Channel 5 News. An all-expense paid trip to New York for a brief appearance on a TV Show soon followed. It was such a shock to visually see and hear what had happened to us right before our own eyes replayed on TV! -----*They reported "**Everything all up in smoke!**"* ***However, that was honestly so disheartening to hear all over again.***

I was working so hard to recover what was lost! I just thanked God for the hearts ***and minds that HE turned to help US!*** I thanked **HIM** that we can share and retell some of this story right NOW for such a time as THIS! ***That old SMOKE is starting to clear more every day!*** Everything has a "season and a reason"! I know that God spoke his WORD to me, and he is using our Family to be a witness of learning how to ***"plough through hard times".*** ***Are you WILLING to hear and understand OUR STORY? Sharing is caring! After years, and years after the Fire***, I had been repairing credit, and getting more educated. I even began buying dirt to lay the foundation for their new home construction on a five acres tract of land to build our first home. Although I did not build yet, I bought a house and made it ***our own saving and buying things for our house a little at a time!*** My children and I have learned so much by taking all of these baby steps to begin a new life. The children, especially the younger ones had begun to get so very impatient during that period of our lives for a new house that still was not built, but who could blame them. I did spend money to have the blueprints designed and three copies were printed. I had approached a Bank in Alexandria using a reputable Builder that the Bank was familiar with, but still they did not approve my plans stating that the same reputable Builder which I solicited on my own could not actually build the size house I had designed for money they approved me for! There was clearly a monopoly going on within the city banks in Alexandria, Louisiana and I was not the only one who saw it, but could not do a thing about it! It is my opinion that if the branch manager, or loan officer did not want to approve a Home loan, your dream will shut down quick even now, as a single "Woman of Color" HA! HA!" Does that remind you of something? Remember when I shared the Story previously about my Grandma Arizona in the past with her bank a century ago? Today, the same similar things are still happening with banks and lending, if you let it get you down! DO NOT STOP MOVING FORWARD! ***We needed our own!*** My children saw that I had helped others to find and purchase their homes as a REALTOR, but I still had many other roadblocks with credit and lack of money for our own home! **I finally found a house already built and visible!** I soon realized there was a ***spiritual warfare going on*** with my finances and building a credit score to build our new house designed by God. I am very happy to announce that the Credit Score is above 750 to date! In the natural, the children wanted their own brand new house and their own bed to sleep in, and so did I. I kept reciting, ***"With God all things are possible".*** We just needed it to happen lots faster. **Remember you will receive what he has for you one way or another, but *you may have to withstand a test of time*, so stay busy doing *GOOD while you are waiting*!** I had to remain calm and not get anxious, or *I probably would have literally lost my mind again! Spiritually* I had to stay around people of like mind.... ***NOT* angry people** and ***NOT* constant complainers!** I needed to be around people who knew how to ***'fight the good fight of faith'*** as mentioned in the Bible, as I had already completed my long-suffering and was into patience! My friends, if you are willing to find solutions for anger and problems, I do suggest you find the scriptures and **God's Promises** to recite and teach your children to stand firm on the Word of God as well, despite what is seen with their own eyes naturally. My children did not understand then where or how fast money goes on bills, and how much was actually spent and needed to live on. My children are not perfect, nor I. They are all very smart, and they have had a few encounters with others that I am NOT proud of, but mistakes happen! Mistakes can also push you and cause more personal growth, **so keep praying your children overcome all obstacles! Continue to strive for a better direction without the repeat of unfavorable behavior.** Financial needs and matters do increase as children grow older. **Why this story I tell? Why these rhymes we tell?** You need to hear truths! No one really understands unless they have been through the same scenes or personally know someone who has a similar story. There are countless others out there. Things happen to ordinary people like us, and they still happen to the rich and famous. **No one is immune!** Our God has and will continue to make us rich through **HIS Blessings**, and *HE* will add no sorry to it because I do believe in HIM and must tell it! **The scripture for this confession is Proverbs 10:22; The Blessings of the Lord brings wealth and adds no trouble to it.** There is someone else out there who needs more hope today, so I had to tell my Story. Please share my story with them! Yes, the devil does still try to steal, kill and destroy your dreams, marriages, children, and your money to mess with your finances, **but He must stop all of his maneuvers now, in Jesus' Name**! Yes, others may come to help for a time, and then those others will definitely leave you all alone once more. **Fight back! Talk to people! Keep pushing forward! Get your eyes on the prize! The Good News is to *Trust in God and Hold on!* God will show you your end, which will be your new beginning! *ASK HIM!***

As a Christian, you are set apart to work on becoming more righteous in the eyes of GOD. ***It is up to you to try to stay that way once you are "born again". There are trials when the Thief comes! As a Christian, you still walk through the Fire, and believe by Faith that the Fire will not burn you COMPLETELY! So, dust the Ashes off! Renew your Mind! Again,*** **The Fire was our new beginning. You need to make whatever your *Fire* is in your *LIFE* right now, your NEW beginning too!** May I also say that for those whose family members did actually die in their FIRE, I am so very sorry! **I pray you continue to trust in GOD and find hope, help, love, and laughter TODAY!**

The Definition of Fire

From Fire to Flame

My definition of a *FIRE* is an intense uncontrolled enthusiasm to consume materials of all kinds with a heated chemical passion and a release of flame. It is a fact that *Fire* does not care whose fuel or oxygen it consumes. A dictionary definition states that a ***Fire*** is a noun. It is a state, or process of unstable combustion in which fuel or material is ignited and combined with oxygen, giving off light, heat, and flame. It is a fact that ***Fire*** causes damage whenever and wherever it goes to forests, homes, other building, other areas, and human life.

A Natural Tip

The most important thing you can do for yourself, as a renter or homeowner, in the event of *a Fire* or any other disaster is to be covered with an insurance policy. Create a Home Inventory List of your personal possessions. Take photos of all of your possessions of value, which will include your clothing, food in refrigerator, and furniture then, store the digital photos or receipts online, or in an album of some sort. I have discovered a lot of information I needed to know years ago, which could have made our lives somewhat easier!

Listen to the News! The Holiday Season from ***November to January*** tends to bring on more fires! After a Fire disaster, find an organization like the Red Cross and other local Community

Centers that can provide Emergency shelter, food, and clothing. **ASK about any Government Agencies** who can offer assistance for rebuilding, and local charities that may offer help organize a fundraiser to support the Family. Additional counseling services may be available, as well to help people cope emotionally for the aftermath of a Fire! (We needed this service, but I did not think about it until NOW, nor were many of these services suggested to me by anyone else, so allow me to share **NOW**!) The Fire Department in your Area will usually be able to supply and install any available free smoke detectors on each floor of your house if you cannot afford to buy them. Call and ask them, then schedule a time for them to come to your house. Once installed, test the smoke detectors regularly and replace the batteries at least one a year, if possible!

A Spiritual Tip

The most important thing you can do for yourself as a Human, in the event of *a Fire*, or any other disaster is to cover yourself with something other than real insurance; called *the Blood of Jesus*! (*You simply say physically, "I COVER myself and my family with the "Blood of Jesus as protection against ALL dangers!")* Create a HOME of worship and praise. Take a mental photo image of yourself and your loved ones standing inside the strong arms of Jesus as **FREE** persons, and be cleared of all your old baggage that you left behind. Be ready to move **FORWARD! *Do not allow things from the past trap your mind. Use positive Self-Talk...Move forward! Move forward! Move Forward!***

Biblical Citings About Fire

Are You At Risk?

Are you at risk of having a fire? Make a Self-Assessment! A Fire to the average eye is usually, and only associated with despair and destruction. The Spiritual Eye sees ***Fire as a Fire***; a method of consuming consecration for a divine intervention of New Beginnings. ***God and Fire are one in the same*** *in a Spiritual sense.*

Please note some of the scriptural references shared, as God manifested Himself on various occasions in the form of ***Fire.*** These manifestations may be seen as He made a Covenant with Abraham in **Genesis 15:17**. The Burning Bush in **Exodus 3:2-4,** The Pillar of ***Fire*** in **Exodus 13:21**, on Mount Sinai in **Exodus 19:18**, in the Flame on the Altar in **Judges 13:20**, and as God answered by ***Fire*** in **1 Kings 18:24, 38**. The ***Fire*** has had many Biblical purposes. I have come to see these facts through reading about ***Fire*** for my own purpose so that I might gain more insight to my own personal mishap. I have learned that ***Fire*** came down from the Heavens to this Earth. ***Fire*** was used to make sacrifices, and to bake bread. ***Fire*** is mentioned to destroy and correct evil. Lastly, ***Fire*** is used as a direct manifestation of God himself! ***Glory, Glory, Glory!*** I know without a shadow of a doubt that when the ***Fire*** started in our rental house between the 2 AM to 3 AM hour, that God was revealing his ***Glory and Deliverance for me and my children.*** I had prayed and cried to God, as I squatted on my knees while on the bathroom floor, that very night after I finished bathing my two younger children the night before, pleading and asking Him for his help and deliverance. I never imagined that **HE** would come in the form of *the Fire* to us! We had **NO** choice but to start over!

Now for your benefit, I did *NOT* come to this conclusion right away! We were devastated, at that time to see a real *Fire* burn all of our belongs. We felt alone, at that time. We felt ashamed to be without the things that we were accustomed to, at that time. We were also reborn and baptized at that time as a new Family, and we still had one another other! Others began to share stories with me about their loved ones who did not live through *their Fire*. *"YES! We did survive! YES! We were scared! ...And Yes! We were all alive and NOT Dead! **Hallelujah!**"*

On Which Side of The Fire Are You?

NOW I wonder on which side of the Fire are you? Choose a side! Are you still in your *Fire,* or out of one? Is there **a *Fire in YOU*** that needs to ***ignite in YOU***, or is there a **Fire** that you ***want put out for YOU?*** Is your *Fire* In *a Heaven or a Hell?* In other words, have you had too many negative things in this World imparted into your Spirit Man causing you to see only the *Fire* of Destruction and Hell? Are you lukewarm to the ideals and standards of Jesus, or are you rejoicing and still on *Fire* for God? I use to wonder why it is so hard for some people to **receive *Jesus freely*** and others not so easy. Then, I had a DREAM! **If you ask God, things are revealed to YOU eventually! *Be Patient! It IS hard to wait!*** I also looked for a Scripture relating to my Dream, and I found the Scripture relating to my Dream. He showed me that the person in my Dream was like being a ***Passerby*** in a very hot dry dessert. I was in a Jeep riding swiftly through rows and rows of those dry hot high rolling white sands in my Dream. I stopped to ask a Passerby if he wanted a ride with me instead of walking because I knew he would never make it out of that desert alive and I really wanted to help him. Unfortunately, he could not see me or hear me. **(He was like a Blind man and a Mute, but he really was neither. He just could not see or hear ME because he was *Spiritually blind!*)** God told me to just pray for him. ***The Passerby could not see me!*** No matter how I tried to help give him a lift, he was Spiritually deaf and blinded, so he just kept on trying to walk those rolling hills of hot sand until exhaustion, then DEATH! My thoughts about that person I said to myself was, ***"What a stubborn FOOL!"*** I was like, **"Wow!"** I felt so sad that I could not help him.

He simply refused the HELP! YOU may know someone like that! ***YOUR job is to continue to pray for yourself and others until that wrong bad spirit shakes loose from them to see and hear you offer them help!*** YOU just simply ask God to come in and help YOU pick up the pieces of your life, so you can be a **BLESSING** to others ***even if you do not have the full total understanding right now of everything that happens to You, and your loved ones. Act in FAITH and OBEDIENCE to what you just read! Start somewhere with YOUR PAGE NUMBER ONE of YOUR LIFE!*** Start to read the Bible a few minutes a day, then work up to an Extended Plan. I was already on ***Fire* for God** when the ***Fire*** came, as I wanted to know more and more about God's Plan for my children, His ways, and myself at that time. I later realized that I actually tested GOD! I promise you I cried out to HIM on my squatted knees the very night before our real ***Fire actually occurred and started blazing!*** Now, ***I feel I am "Fireproofed", but trials may still come!*** I feel as though I am one who ***escaped*** to tell **YOU today.....There is hope! Do YOU hear me? *THERE IS HOPE FOR YOU and Your Family!* There is GOD's Grace! *My "full circle" of rebirth is being completed daily right now!*** The life that we live on this Earth is a test of your relationship with God and the others around you! Many may not hear you but MANY WILL! **People in your Inner Circle DO Matter!** Fulfilling your purpose in life will mean that you will not completely be alone, as you climb the ladder. You must connect some kind of way with somebody or others. YOU ARE HUMAN! **YOU have something different to offer someone than I do! YOU are to share of yourself for something good! *YOU ARE NOT ALONE! You do not HAVE TO BE ALONE!* LOVE God and Yourself FIRST! *FIND OUT WHO YOU ARE!***

The Choice is Yours

The Choice is Yours! That Choice is the hardest part to choose because we get so very busy with living LIFE in this life of daunting daily tasks! For example, I started this Book immediately after the ***Fire*** and had a true desire to write this Book immediately, so that I would not forget things. I could not complete the writing or thoughts for this Book until right **NOW, which is YEARS LATER!** There is so much more pressure on you when you are Single. Being Single is nice too in the beginning of your Young Adult Stage of Life. It has its part to play in growing up, and learning how to overcome obstacles until you are ready to share your life with another person. I had to live, work, and help care for my grandmother Arizona, care for myself, care for my children, help other kids as Teacher, provide food to eat as "Head of Household", buy a house, get furniture, pay bills, plan, and search for printers and publishing companies and ideas, etc!, etc, etc! **My "Things to Do List" goes On-and-On-and ON! You know the deal!** I wrote down bits and pieces over the years, and I always knew that the task of completing our Story in a Book Form would be accomplished one day because the **desire to write, and share the ideas** given for the Book was already placed years ago in my Heart ***by HIM from the very beginning due to the FIRE!*** Praise be to God it is so completed NOW! My Friends, ***"Rekindle your Flame"*** let the ***Fire of the Living God reign in your Heart and Soul TODAY!***

Poetry Selections by the Family as Fire Victims

The Fireflies Dance

I am calling this Section of my Book the "Fireflies Dance"! This is a "Poetic Justice" of the effects of being the Fire victim after falling into a "Night Battle" with a Fire, and the "Morning Victory" from the flight of a Fire as seen by my children, and myself through poetry. I want to reiterate that we are molded, and imprinted by God. *We are truly made in His image.* Who knows... It may or may not take a Fire to remold and reshape YOUR life. Just please find some good out of your mishaps regardless of what it is; whether you have, or whether you have NOT! *We are all designed to CREATE and be CREATIVE! ...so, CREATE and be CREATIVE! Please find a positive way to release your pain and hardship! I pray you enjoy these original Poems written by my Children and Niece!*

THE NIGHTMARE THAT CAME TRUE by Alex

The Fire

"You have no authority you devil; I am covered in the Blood."

"Yeah, take that now! You know that I'm loved."

I sleep so peacefully only to awaken to my worst nightmare.

A house fire of great proportion, smoke here and smoke over there.

I heard, "Get up Lex, the house is on FIRE!"

Half asleep, I did not even know what my brother was talking about that

was so dire.

I did not realize then, but I soon was to find out.

What in the world is that smell," Oh no it's smoke. No doubt, Get out!

All I knew was one thing…grab my Jordan tennis shoes and Go, Go, Go so I

would not choke!

My Mom yells, "I need my purse, but there is so much smoke!"

I ran back inside the house to see if I could find my mother's possession.

I did not care about any diminishing air obsession.

I returned from our flaming house with no such luck.

Now I realize back then I was truly, "One Brave Young Buck."

Black, smeared, burnt were now the words, which characterized our house

on the news.

That afternoon and all I can think was... MY SHOES!

God give me the strength to show my face the next day at school.

A FACE OF PERIL By Austen

In the shadows of the night, where nightmares unfold,
I awoke to a tale of a fire and a hero untold.
The crackling whispers of danger near,
A dance of flames, and awakening fear.

The stench of burnt marshmallows and smoke filled the air,
Silent sirens echoed in my heart knowing danger was near.
As I sprang to life, urging everyone to wake as the smoke swirls,
For my mother and siblings, are the center of my world.

In the hush of embers, mom screams grab what we can,
For the memories in that home won't ever be seen again.
A Lullaby of danger, a flickering song.
Who knew a strong family is what we had all along.

We were touched by God, as he guided our escapes,
In the face of peril, we found our capes.
From the streets we watched, in our minds uncertainty resides,
At least we were safe, standing side by side.

Tender hands grasped in the cloak of night,
A family's bond, a beacon of light.
Through the ashes we emerged, in all our entire,
A tale of awakening escaping the fire!

INTENSE by Austen

Intense heat of orange to red hue

Flames of yellow and blue

All consumed in its path

Faith only does I hath

FIRE IN THE NIGHT by Austen

Pitch black with not much to see,

A strange stench approaches me,

The smell grew louder as the suspense grew,

Oh what should one in my predicament do?

Check the hall and check the kitchen,

Next, the room where the light does glisten,

Smoke fills the air and burns my eyes,

What is this light next to the bed where my family lies?

Get up! Get up! I scream in fear,

Everyone needs to get out of here,

Sizzle and crackle the fire roars,

Grasp what you can and sprint to the doors,

Into the night sky we escape in luck,

What if I would not have woken up?

This would cause everything to go amuck!

I stand and watch as the flames destroy the lumber,

Of what was once my home and place of slumber?

WHAT IS FIRE by Asa

What is Fire?

The sight of fire

Has no desire

Fire kills, destroys, and burns

But with God

One has no concern.

A WORLD OF FIRE by Ayanna

My world is burning down

As the flames rise higher

Sadness can always be found

In the destruction of fire

INSPIRE FIRE by Abram

What is FIRE?

Fire is HOT

Fire does not STOP

Fire is MEAN

Fire quickly comes on the SCENE

What is FIRE?

Fire can INSPIRE

Fire has that red GLOW

I KNOW.

THE ROOF IS ON FIRE by Abram

I was in my house

My mom was in a blouse

Everyone was sleep

You couldn't hear a peep

I was little

I was still counting sheep

1, 2, 3, 4...Here comes the fire knock at my door.

5, 6, 7, 8...I am so sleepy the fire rises from the floor.

Luckily my brother woke up 'cause it was not my time to go to heaven!

WHAT I THINK ABOUT FIRE by Abi

*Written at age 7

What I think about....

Fire is in the past

It can....

Even break glass.

My auntie's home got

Burned by fire and now

She is living even higher.

My Auntie needs to try to get more money

Most of all...

... She can still make me laugh. She is still funny.

WHAT I THINK ABOUT FIRE by Abi

*Written at age 21

Before the sun rose with its glorious rays,

The little morning star was held captive in space.

An invisible chain had pulled her light years away

From her small, cozy home that had begun to fray.

The chain seemed to tighten the closer the little morning star got

To the giant, dead earth that stood frozen on the spot.

At once the little morning star finally understood her use.

The commander of the invisible chain wanted to use

Her as a sacrificial flame.

An eternal flame that gives without taking,

That consumes without destroying,

That heats without burning,

That dies without living.

Yes, the commander wanted to use her as a sacrifice

To the cold dead earth.

But what is sacrifice without choice?

The little morning star felt her heart scream in pain

And silently wished that she had strong wings to fly her away.

Far away from the pain, away from the chain, and far, far away

From what everybody else could gain.

Only the chain remained.

Despite the hope she carried in her heart,

The little morning star never got her wings to fly,

And her light died a little inside.

A SELECTION OF Poems By ANDREA

Dance Through The Fire

Fire to flame. Loss of desire. Destroyer of all.

See the crumpling charred walls and the burnt ash

Dance through the Fire

Fire to flame. Loss of desire. Destroyer of all.

See the years of production flee with the need for more cash

Dance through the Fire

Fire to flame. Loss of desire. Destroyer of all.

Someone please help me to dance.

The tables will turn

Fire to flame. You are not mine alone.

FIRE Is Torture

Hope, faith, and love

Cries to the heavenly Father above

Restore and remove all doubt

Fire is torture

Thank you, thank you for getting me out

Of a time that caused great pain

Fire is torture

Plenty to lose and much to gain

Faith, love and hope remain!

MEMORIES Of Fire

Dancing smoke-filled air

Memories that harbor worry and care

Float my mind to whimper and tear

Sink me in weathering passions so unclear

Smell of burn

Sounds of spurn

Lingers on…

Fire is torture no more

Just memories to explore

And life to adore

THE FIREFLIES Dance in the Dark

We dance, we sing, we hope

Bundles of bandaged dreams

Things really do not appear, as they seem

Stripped of a humanity with cares

Vanished tables and wares

Brought from the dark to the light of solitude

Blown into prayer and God's attitude

No Space For Defense

A Louisiana flight and no defense during the night

Suppression

Depression

Aggression

A Louisiana southern hospitality and a common sight

Suppression

Depression

Aggression

Dancing Fireflies like me

Into God's majesty

No need for pretense

No space for defense

Truth be told, "A Fire Arose From My Soul!"

DANCE QUICKLY INTO A NEW BEGINNING!!!

Learn About Fire!

Fire is natural part and a hot spot

With increase of damage that burns

Caution controlled is a difficult lot

Ignited gash of learned concerns

Learn baby learn

Burn baby burn

Learn baby LEARN!

Fire Is Natural

A Natural heat and light to the world

A heart-pumping stir of emotions twirled

A very useful property to humankind

A plan devised by God the mastermind

A fire disaster creates much fear

A fire disaster lasts from year to year

A fire can be used as an instrument of destruction

A fire from Heaven can be a cleansing clearing function

Pray for your enemies on a bent knee to start

Pray for the sick and rekindle your heart

Your fire need not be of vengeance or wrath

Rather your fire may be a God given chosen path

And God's mercy endures forever and ever and ever...

Tongues Of Fire

Tongues of Fire, where be you

Tongues of Fire bring light through and through

Open your mouth and be not scared of man

Open your mouth and speak throughout this land

The Fire caused thousands to die throughout the land

The Fire of God also brought much increase to man

Speak your Tongues

What Fire Brings

One Fire brings death

One Fire brings life

One Fire bring health

One Fire brings strife

Water alone cannot quench the fire....Indeed Fire is a continuous battle

FIRE, Get My Attention

Fire, draw my attention to where it ought to be

Fire, draw my attention, I want to be free

Fire makes you notice the things of the past

Fire makes you notice that material things do not last

There is no need to wrestle with your own desire

Fire is static. It moves. It keeps you warm. It is FIRE!

Rise O' Fire

Elements of heat that move on and on

Elements of heat that rise during night until crack of dawn

Rise ole elements of heat

See a new Heaven on Earth

See a new heat wave be birthed

Come forth! Rise o' Fire!

RISE!

Fire Is Light

Now, I see myself in a completely different light

I am now in a cleansing purified fire flight

I dance through the dark in the light of my God

Who loves me unconditionally; we are like little peas in a pod

As long as man uses bombs and fire for destruction

Our lands will not be healed, nor used for its spiritual function

God's love within me wants to bring peace, hope and laughter to all

Humankind

God's fire breeds much, much peace of mind until the end of time.

The Fire System

Man systems of laws, customs, and thoughts for school

When Man's system of punishment and ridicule rule

Fire brings much fear to Man

God's way of Laws are flawed with customs, and thoughts for school

When God's way of justice and mercy and grace rule

Fire brings light to Man

Fear God and his Fire System!

Arose the Flame

Arose the flame from the light of night

Arose the smoke from the helter of shelter

Arose the fire from gentle sneeze of breeze

Arose the burns of disaster from the Master

And His hands are lifted up and made known; Taberah

Tongues of Fire

Watch your tongue,

It is a blazing fire with no recourse

Watch your tongue

It was designed to uplift with no remorse

Watch your tongue

Rejoice and be glad

Burn with a desire to be pleasing not mad

A fiery tongue brings forth rage

A joyful tongue releases you from your cage

Holy Spirit, engage

Fall on us with your "Tongues of Fire"

Now, stand prepared for anything

Let your voices ring

FIRE ABLAZE

"Pictures frame real words beyond your Imagination."

Charred and Burnt Area of Room

FIRE ABLAZE

"Pictures frame real words beyond your Imagination."

Piles of Burnt Belongings in Bedroom

FIRE ABLAZE

"Pictures frame real words beyond your Imagination."

Piles of Burnt Belongings

FIRE ABLAZE

"Pictures frame real words beyond your Imagination."

Oldest Son Alex going thru the Rubbish left in his Bedroom in Photo

<u>FIRE ABLAZE</u>

"Pictures frame real words beyond your Imagination."

Andrea and her Children
"Day 1 - *After The Fire*"

From Left to Right: Top Row - Austen, Andrea, Alex, Asa
Bottom Row - Ayanna, Abram

FIRE ABLAZE

"Pictures frame real words beyond your Imagination."

Andrea and Children: Austen, Andrea, Asa, Abram, Ayanna, and Alex after the Repast of Andrea's Dad; "Chico" Anderson Wardsworth, Jr.

FIRE ABLAZE

"Pictures frame real words beyond your Imagination."

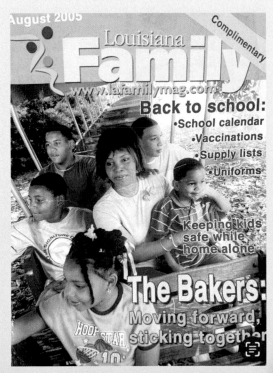 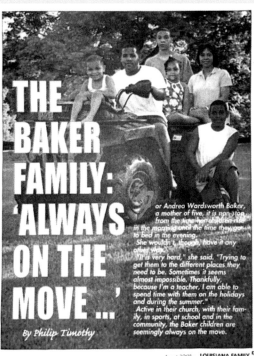

Article about the Family in THE LOUISIANA FAMILY Magazine
https://imagn.com/setImages/549815/preview/22161738
Aug 1, 2005; Alexandria, LA, USA; Louisiana Family
Magazine cover: Meet the Baker Family; [CAPTION]
ATTRIBUTION: © The Town Talk – USA TODAY NETWORK

_____

Phillip Timothy; The Baker Family: Always On The Move; The Louisiana Family Magazine; August 2005.

FIRE ABLAZE

"Pictures frame real words beyond your Imagination."

Sixteen-year-old Alex, an honor student in the Medical Magnet Program at Peabody, is participating in a math and science program at Wiley College in Marshall, Texas, this summer. Planning on becoming anesthetist, he is trying to earn college credits for when he goes to college in two years.

Fifteen-year-old Austen, all of 6-foot-3, is also an honor student in the Engineering Magnet Program at Peabody and is involved in the AAU Boys Basketball League in Opelousas and Peabody Magnet's Summer League Basketball program.

Nine-year-old Asa, a fifth-grader at Phoenix Magnet Elementary, is the most intense and is involved in basketball, football and baseball. Last year he was selected as the 2004 Defensive MVP in the AAA Flag Football League and competes in the Kappa Basketball League.

Seven-year-old Ayanna, the only girl in the family, also attends Phoenix Magnet Elementary and finished with straight As in every subject.

While she loves to read, play computer games and go swimming, she is participating in dance lessons this summer with Vicki's Dance Studio.

Four-year-old Abram, better known as "Bam Bam," is the youngest of the Bakers. Full of play and a dabbling of mischief, he is the 'character' of the family. Having successfully completed the Cenla Community Action Head Start Program, he will be attending Peabody Montessori this year.

"We're just one big, happy family," Andrea said. "They keep me young, especially 'Bam Bam.' We love to spend time together, watch movies, go out to eat and visit the grandparents in Lecompte or visit my 98-year-old grandmother (the children's great grandmother) every Sunday."

But the Bakers' togetherness took on a new meaning in late October, around 2:15 a.m. when Austen, then 14, smelled smoke and awakened Andrea where she and her two youngest children were sleeping.

Fire destroyed their three-bedroom home and fire department officials said it was caused by an electrical fire, which

Continued Article about Andrea and her Family in THE LOUISIANA FAMILY Magazine https://imagn.com/setImages/549815/preview/22161738 **Aug 1, 2005; Alexandria, LA, USA; Louisiana Family Magazine cover: Meet the Baker Family; [CAPTION] ATTRIBUTION: © The Town Talk – USA TODAY NETWORK**

Phillip Timothy; The Baker Family: Always On The Move; The Louisiana Family Magazine; August 2005, Page 6.

FIRE ABLAZE

"Pictures frame real words beyond your Imagination."

**Continued Article about THE FAMILY in
THE LOUISIANA FAMILY Magazine** https://imagn.com/setImages/549815/
preview/22161738 **Aug 1, 2005; Alexandria, LA, USA; Louisiana
Family Magazine cover: Meet the Baker Family; [CAPTION]
ATTRIBUTION: © The Town Talk – USA TODAY NETWORK**

*Phillip Timothy; The Baker Family: Always On The Move; The Louisiana Family
Magazine; August 2005.*

FIRE ABLAZE

"Pictures frame real words beyond your Imagination."

Family loses everything in house fire

By Mandy M. Goodnight
The Town Talk

Raymond Jones with Matt's Janitor Service tosses a shovel of debris into a trash bin located inside a gutted Redwood Street house. The Baker family lost everything they own in the fire. — Paul Rutherford/The Town Talk

Andrea Wardsworth Baker watched as her children wandered through the remains of their belongings.

Asa, 9, and Ayanna, 6, found a set a golf clubs among the rubble. Like typical children, they fought over the only toy they had.

"There is very little left," Baker said.

The single mother of five lost her house to fire on Saturday.

On Tuesday, the charred remains of furniture, carpet, clothing and appliances were piled into the front yard of the Redwood Street residence.

Workers with Matt's Janitor Service were inside, cleaning what they could.

On the outside, Baker could barely stand to look at what was left of her belongings.

Alexandria Fire Department officials said an electrical fire started in Baker's bedroom, where she and her two youngest children were sleeping.

Fourteen-year-old Austen awakened his mother about 2 a.m. Saturday. He had smelled smoke.

"We are lucky that he woke us up, otherwise ...," she said not finishing the thought.

The Peabody Magnet High School special education teacher has moved her family in with relatives.

Neighbors and her church have given them some clothing and other donations. The American Red Cross also has provided vouchers for some purchases.

A Red Cross spokeswoman said Wednesday that the shelter helps with emergency needs for families and individuals involved in a disaster. The assistance given depends on the needs of the disaster victims.

A helping hand

To help with disaster relief in Cenla, donations may be made to the American Red Cross. For information, call (318) 442-6621. To help the family, donations may be made to them and The Word Christian Center of Alexandria at any Hibernia Bank location.

Faculty and students at Peabody Magnet High School are collecting money to help Baker and her family.

The family did have some insurance.

Baker said she has to get uniforms for her four school-age children: Two attend Peabody Magnet High School, and two are enrolled at Phoenix Magnet Elementary School. Baker also needs clothing so that she can return to work.

"We ran out of the house with nothing but nightclothes on," Baker said.

She tried to go back into the burning structure to find her purse and car keys, but the smoke was too much.

Besides practical items, Baker lost pictures, scrapbooks and the journals she kept on each of her children.

"Those are things I can't get back," she said. "They are just gone."

As she spoke, Baker's father, Anderson Wardsworth, walked past, shaking his head. "It is hard to believe this happened," he said.

Mandy M. Goodnight: 487-6465; mgoodnight@thetowntalk.com

Article Clippings about ANDREA and THE FAMILY
https://www.newspapers.com/article/the-town-talk/136095936/
October 22, 2004 - Family loses everything in House Fire by Mandy M. Goodnight
ATTRIBUTION: © The Town Talk — USA TODAY NETWORK

Mandy M. Goodnight, *Family Loses Everything in House Fire;* The Town Talk, Friday, October 22, 2004: Section A3

<u>FIRE ABLAZE</u>

"Pictures frame real words beyond your Imagination."

**Article about THE FAMILY in Local CENLA TOWN TALK Newspaper)
January 9, 2005 – Makeover - Fire Victim to be on National TV
Show** https://www.newspapers.com/article/the-town-talk/136096133/

ATTRIBUTION: © The Town Talk – USA TODAY NETWORK

Eugene Sutherland; *Fire Victim to be National TV Show;* **The Town Talk, Sunday,
January 9, 2005: Section A**

FIRE ABLAZE

"Pictures frame real words beyond your Imagination."

The Homemade Dessert for Gift Donations

- **Banana Pudding**
- **Chocolate cake with Pecan Topping**
- **Butter Pineapple with Pecan Topping**

FIRE ABLAZE

"Pictures frame real words beyond your Imagination."

Andrea and her five children Baptized on March 27, 2005

<u>FIRE ABLAZE</u>

"Pictures frame real words beyond your Imagination."

(The Louisiana Family Sample Essay Written for the Contest Entry)
Andrea entered this essay in late night after 11:00 PM
for the Louisiana Family Magazine Essay Contest offered
through the Alexandria Town Talk on 04/02/2005.

THE QUESTION: What Does Being a Family Mean to You?

"What Being A Family Means To Us"

Humankind is our family. United we stand. Our Nation's strength is related to our family's strength. Children usually follow the examples of their parents. We do pass on family blessings and must build relationships and assume responsibility to care for one another in good times and bad times. We must seek good counsel and guidance when we do not know how to handle situations before we send our children out to face the world. Every family has their own troubles, but one of God's greatest resources is the Family! Jesus adopts us all into HIS family, and guess what? One faithful parent can affect the world starting with the family of God has already given to you!

We children are of a blend mix of Black and Indian American Family. I am a divorced parent whose children live with me. I am a Teacher by profession, and a mom of five wonderfully and handsomely made children of four sons and one beautiful daughter. We invited their Daddy to church this past Easter Sunday, as we realized that we all did chose adoption by Jesus and we wanted to witness showering the love of God through our *water baptism* at our church, The Word Christian Center. Our lives have been through many difficulties. Realize many lower middle-income families have good times and bad for whatever reasons, but we have always enjoyed the company of one another. In mid-October of 2004, we awoke to smoke filled air and burning curtains by the bed in our small three-bedroom rental house. This lead to the invasion of a thief called "Fire"! This "Fire" destroyed everything we had and held dear to us. As we looked through our charred remains the next day, it became clear that our chances of ever obtaining a bigger house with at least two acres of land and a better way of life seemed very distant in our near future. All of a sudden, my family, as we knew it, no longer had a boundary within the walls of a small three-bedroom one-bath rental house. Our family now had grown to be our neighbors, the church, the school, and others whom we did not know in the community of our Alexandria hometown, through the love of God. We had no idea how important a life could be, and how the relationships you establish with others on an everyday basis can mean so much. Our eyes were open to how God wants us to love one another and not forget those who have less than we have. *Do not allow a day to go without sharing some of God's goodness with someone, whether it be money, land, a smile, a meal, a ride, a walk, a talk, a flower, or a note of praise to anyone...to everyone...even to those whom you would not consider your friend or relative—even your enemy!* We have always loved one another enough to spend a lot of time together. We enjoyed the crawfish boils at the in-laws house, watching movies, going out to eat, participating in sports, family chores, reading the bible together periodically, and visiting our ninety-eight year old grandmother, Arizona in Pineville, Louisiana, faithfully on Sundays. That was our simple life. *Time* was one investment God had always instilled in me, as a parent, to provide to the children. There has always been teachable moments to help the children learn about ones who misuse you, steal from you, talk about you, not share with you, or offer help when needed. *However, the early morn of the Fire really taught us all that Jesus could put out any fire in your life. He whispered, "Water!"* As living water, HE will give you the love and faith your family needs. We do not want to mislead you into thinking that everything is perfect because it NEVER has been, and may NEVER be. We still have needs. Our family has extended into the home of my parents' home. We are still waiting on our house and land to make OUR HOME. We still have financial, emotional, physical, and mental issues to deal with on a daily basis while much physical rest is needed. It has always been a battle to listen to the needs and desires of five of your own children who call your name fifty-plus times a day. Then listen to the concerns of others' children as well as a teacher, and stay fresh every morning, after staying up until 12:30 PM or 1:00 AM the next morning to complete the day's chores to keep things moving forward. I am still so amazed and in awe that we are all still here ALIVE! Every day is so beautiful! We can smell the flowers, we can feel the wind, we can breathe the air, we can feel the pain, we can fuss and try not to cuss, we can feel the warmth of a hug and a kiss, and we do love one another and our neighbors. We can teach one another to fall to our knees, praise our Lord, and thank him for his son, Jesus; the one person who loves us all so much. He died, so that we may be adopted into HIS Family.

What does being a family mean? The early morn of the fire really taught us ALL that Jesus could put out any fire in your life, as the living water, and give you the hope your family needs. It means learning to live everyday more pleasing to God, so keep practicing! We want to love more, and we invite you to live and love for Jesus with us! You are adopted into our new family. It is up to you. We are one nation under God and indivisible.

Thank you for this opportunity!

Andrea Wardsworth Baker & Family

Sincerely,

Andrea, Alex, Austen, Asa, Ayanna & Abram

FIRE ABLAZE

"Pictures frame real words beyond your Imagination."

Andrea & Alex, Our Hero Who Reentered The Burning House to Find His Mom's Purse!

Andrea & Asa

<u>FIRE ABLAZE</u>

"Pictures frame real words beyond your Imagination."

Andrea & Ayanna

Andrea & Abram

FIRE ABLAZE

"Pictures frame real words beyond your Imagination."

**July 24, 2021 Picture of Andrea's Children at Wedding
Alex, Asa, Ayanna, Ayanna, Abram, Austen**

FIRE ABLAZE

"Pictures frame real words beyond your Imagination."

Abram, Alex, Andrea, & Austen

Andrea & Charles on Wedding Day July 24, 2021
Other Wedding Photos on The Knot: theknot.com/andreabandcharlesb

FIRE ABLAZE

"Pictures frame real words beyond your Imagination."

Andrea's Parents; Mary Louise James & Anderson "Chico" Wardsworth, Jr.

FIRE ABLAZE

"Pictures frame real words beyond your Imagination."

Andrea's Maternal Grandparents; Arizona James & Joseph Freeman James

<u>FIRE ABLAZE</u>

"Pictures frame real words beyond your Imagination."

"Austen, Our "Hero!"
(Andrea's second son; Austen) Austen awakened their Family from their
HOUSE FIRE at 2 AM

FIRE ABLAZE

"Pictures frame real words beyond your Imagination."

**Article about Andrea, the Author in November 2023
Literary Focus Section -THE CENLA FOCUS Magazine Online
Pages 36-37 ATTRIBUTION: www.cenlafocus.com**

FIRE ABLAZE

"Pictures frame real words beyond your Imagination."

visions can be brought to reality, then shared with the world. She loves writing poetry and inspiring others by making life come alive in her books. Andrea's great spirit of understanding sets her apart by capturing the essence of life's ups and downs.

Andrea's writings range from preschool handwriting books and children's books to a variety of self-improvement guides, which include cooking recipes, health, wills, trust, and estate planning. She has written about a "little bit of everything," and all of it is good reading.

Andrea believes strongly, "without strong faith in God, life doesn't mean a thing!" I have enjoyed and been enlightened by examining her unique and informative selection of books which I recommend.

For more information on Andrea and her books, go to her website: www.aroseenterprisesllc.com.

**Continued Article about the Andrea, the Author
THE CENLA FOCUS Magazine November 2023 Issue
Literary Focus Section - Pages 36-37 Online
ATTRIBUTION: www.cenlafocus.com**

Michael Wynne; *Author Andrea Wardsworth Beasley;* **The Cenla Focus Magazine, November, 2023 : Literary Focus Section**

FIREPROOF YOUR HOME WITH THIS CHECKLIST

✓ 1. Install the proper fire alarms and get some fire extinguishers. Ask your neighborhood Fire Department if they can install your fire alarms outside of the bedrooms in the Hallways, or in your bedrooms depending on your current City or County regulations.

✓ 2. Call the nearby Red Cross and ask if they have some fire alarms to give away!

✓ 3. Maintain a good water supply with a few gallons of tap water and actually practice family fire drills.

✓ 4. Use fire-resistant building and roof materials for your home, if building a new home and clear any thick crowded vegetation from around your home.

✓ 5. Use fire-resistant materials wherever you can in an existing home and take photos of your furniture and other valuable items in your home. Place important items in a waterproof and/or fireproof metal box or container.

✓ 6. Sleep in fire resistant pajamas, night gown, or lounge wear.

✓ 7. Develop a Disaster Plan or Evacuation Plan, and post Emergency Numbers in a common area of your home.

✓ 8. Keep all of your important Documents such as Social Security Cards, Birth Certificates, Power of Attorney and other Legal Documents in a metal fire and waterproof box.

✓ 9. Teach your Children to CALL 911!

✓ 10. Pray Together! Teach your children to PRAY!

A Savior of Mercy

ISAIAH 43 *(NIV Bible)*

ISRAEL'S ONLY SAVIOR

¹ But now, this is what the LORD says—

He who created you, Jacob,

He who formed you, Israel:

"Do not fear, for I have redeemed you;

I have summoned you by name; you are mine.

² When you pass through the waters,

I will be with you;

And when you pass through the rivers,

They will not sweep over you.

_When you walk through the fire__,_

You will not be burned;

_The flames will not set you ablaze__._

3 For I am the LORD your God,

The Holy One of Israel, your Savior;

I give Egypt for your ransom,

Cush and Seba in your stead.

4 Since you are precious and honored in my sight,

And because I love you,

I will give people in exchange for you,

Nations in exchange for your life.

[5] Do not be afraid, for I am with you;

I will bring your children from the east

And gather you from the west.

[6] I will say to the north, 'Give them up!'

And to the south, 'Do not hold them back.'

Bring my sons from afar

And my daughters from the ends of the earth—

[7] everyone who is called by my name,

Whom I created for my glory,

Whom I formed and made.

⁸ *Lead out those who have eyes but are blind,*

Who have ears but are deaf.

⁹ All the nations gather together

And the peoples assemble.

Which of their gods foretold this

And proclaimed to us the former things?

Let them bring in their witnesses to prove they were right,

So that others may hear and say, "It is true."

¹⁰ *"You are my witnesses,"* declares the LORD,

"And my servant whom I have chosen,

So that you may know and believe me

And understand that I am he.

Before me, no god was formed,

Nor will there be one after me.

[11] I, even I, am the LORD,

And apart from me there is no savior.

[12] I have revealed and saved and proclaimed—

I, and not some foreign god among you.

You are my witnesses," declares the LORD, "that I am God.

[13] Yes, and from ancient days I am he.

No one can deliver out of my hand.

When I act, who can reverse it?"

God's Mercy and Israel's Unfaithfulness

[14] This is what the LORD says—

Your Redeemer, the Holy One of Israel:

"For your sake, I will send to Babylon

And bring down as fugitives all the Babylonians,

In the ships in which they took pride.

¹⁵ **I am the LORD, your Holy One,**

Israel's Creator, your King."

¹⁶ **This is what the LORD says—**

He who made a way through the sea,

a path through the mighty waters,

¹⁷ **who drew out the chariots and horses,**

The army and reinforcements together,

And they lay there, never to rise again,

Extinguished, snuffed out like a wick:

[18] *"Forget the former things;*

Do not dwell on the past.

[19] *See, I am doing a new thing!*

Now it springs up; do you not perceive it?

I am making a way in the wilderness

And streams in the wasteland.

[20] *The wild animals honor me,*

The jackals and the owls,

Because I provide water in the wilderness

And streams in the wasteland,

To give drink to my people, my chosen,

[21] the people I formed for myself

That they may proclaim my praise.

[22] "Yet you have not called on me, Jacob,

You have not wearied yourselves for me, Israel.

[23] You have not brought me sheep for burnt offerings,

Nor honored me with your sacrifices.

I have not burdened you with grain offerings

Nor wearied you with demands for incense.

²⁴ You have not bought any fragrant calamus for me,

Or lavished on me the fat of your sacrifices.

But you have burdened me with your sins

And wearied me with your offenses.

²⁵ "I, even I, am he who blots out

Your transgressions, for my own sake,

And remembers your sins no more.

²⁶ Review the past for me,

Let us argue the matter together;

State the case for your innocence.

²⁷ Your first father sinned;

Those I sent to teach you rebelled against me.

²⁸ So I disgraced the dignitaries of your temple;

I consigned Jacob to destruction

and Israel to scorn.

---

www.biblegateway.com; Israel's Only Savior; Isaiah 43(NIV) New International Version

My Personal Prayer For You

Dear God, Fireproof US! Ignite our fire and increase our

Productive hands. Help us to stand retardant to any

Flames and corruption in this World.

You have freed your people from all bondage so that

We may walk as your Flames on this Earth. We surrender!

We surrender! Help us to recognize our own brokenness.

Rekindle our Spirit Man, so that we may love, as you love us.

Let that love motivate and help US!

Help us rise above our ashes, and rise seated where you want us to be---

On this Earth and Beyond everywhere we go...

Under your direct Fire of Glory!

Free US! Keep US! In Your Perfect Peace!

AMEN

"May you be "Blessed Abundantly" for the purchase, reading, and sharing of this Book and completely "ARISE From any Fire" in Your LIFE!

We pray for continued blue skies, sunshine, love, laughter, and peace in your life TODAY! Much Love to You and Yours from Our Family."

Sincerely,

~Andrea, Alex, Austen, Asa, Ayanna, and Abram~

<u>A Fire Arose From My Soul</u>

PERSONAL NOTES & THOUGHTS ABOUT THE BOOK

_____

_____

_____

_____

_____

_____

_____

_____

_____

_____

_____

_____

_____

_____

_____

_____

_____

_____

_____

_____

_____

_____

_____

_____

_____

_____

_____

_____

_____

_____

_____

_____

_____

_____

_____

_____

_____

_____

_____

_____

_____

_____ ***Thank you!***

Printed in the United States
by Baker & Taylor Publisher Services